50 Eating Well Everyday Recipes for Home

By: Kelly Johnson

Table of Contents

- Grilled Salmon with Lemon-Dill Sauce
- Quinoa and Black Bean Salad
- Roasted Vegetable Buddha Bowl
- Spinach and Feta Stuffed Chicken Breast
- Mediterranean Chickpea Salad
- Sweet Potato and Kale Hash
- Shrimp and Avocado Lettuce Wraps
- Teriyaki Tofu Stir-Fry
- Lemon Garlic Roasted Chicken Thighs
- Cauliflower Fried Rice
- Blackened Tilapia Tacos
- Caprese Zucchini Noodles
- Turkey and Vegetable Skewers
- Tomato Basil Mozzarella Chicken
- Greek Yogurt Parfait with Berries
- Lentil and Vegetable Soup
- Baked Cod with Herbed Quinoa
- Pesto Pasta with Cherry Tomatoes
- Turkey and Quinoa Stuffed Peppers
- Asian-inspired Salmon Bowl
- Zucchini Noodles with Pesto and Cherry Tomatoes
- Chickpea and Spinach Curry
- Roasted Red Pepper and Hummus Wrap
- Honey Mustard Glazed Salmon
- Spaghetti Squash Primavera
- Chicken and Broccoli Stir-Fry
- Avocado and Black Bean Quesadillas
- Brussels Sprouts and Bacon Hash
- Lemon Herb Grilled Shrimp
- Ratatouille with Quinoa
- Cilantro Lime Chicken Skewers
- Sweet Potato and Black Bean Enchiladas
- Greek Salad with Grilled Chicken
- Teriyaki Vegetable Stir-Fry
- Baked Eggplant Parmesan
- Turkey and Spinach Meatballs
- Quinoa and Kale Stuffed Acorn Squash
- Tuna Salad Lettuce Wraps
- Lemon Rosemary Grilled Swordfish
- Cauliflower and Chickpea Curry

- Pesto Zoodles with Cherry Tomatoes
- Greek Quinoa Salad
- Lemon Garlic Shrimp and Asparagus
- Mexican Cauliflower Rice Bowl
- Roasted Chicken with Brussels Sprouts and Potatoes
- Veggie and Hummus Wrap
- Shrimp and Vegetable Skewers
- Spinach and Artichoke Stuffed Portobello Mushrooms
- Coconut Curry Chicken
- Quinoa and Blackberry Salad

Grilled Salmon with Lemon-Dill Sauce

Ingredients:

For Salmon:

- 4 salmon fillets
- Salt and pepper to taste
- 2 tablespoons olive oil
- 2 teaspoons lemon zest
- 2 tablespoons fresh lemon juice
- 2 teaspoons dried dill (or 2 tablespoons fresh dill, chopped)

For Lemon-Dill Sauce:

- 1/2 cup Greek yogurt
- 1 tablespoon mayonnaise
- 1 tablespoon fresh dill, chopped
- 1 tablespoon capers, drained
- 1 teaspoon Dijon mustard
- Salt and pepper to taste

Instructions:

Preheat the grill to medium-high heat.
Season the salmon fillets with salt and pepper. In a small bowl, mix together olive oil, lemon zest, lemon juice, and dried dill.
Brush the salmon fillets with the lemon-dill mixture, ensuring they are well-coated.
Place the salmon fillets on the preheated grill. Grill for about 4-5 minutes per side, or until the salmon is cooked through and easily flakes with a fork.
While the salmon is grilling, prepare the Lemon-Dill Sauce. In a bowl, combine Greek yogurt, mayonnaise, fresh dill, capers, Dijon mustard, salt, and pepper. Mix well.
Once the salmon is done, remove it from the grill and place it on serving plates.
Drizzle the Lemon-Dill Sauce over the grilled salmon or serve it on the side as a dipping sauce.
Garnish with additional fresh dill and lemon slices if desired.

This Grilled Salmon with Lemon-Dill Sauce is a delicious and light dish that's perfect for a healthy everyday meal. Enjoy!

Quinoa and Black Bean Salad

Ingredients:

For the Salad:

- 1 cup quinoa, rinsed and cooked according to package instructions
- 1 can (15 oz) black beans, drained and rinsed
- 1 cup corn kernels (fresh, frozen, or canned)
- 1 cup cherry tomatoes, halved
- 1 red bell pepper, diced
- 1/2 red onion, finely chopped
- 1/4 cup fresh cilantro, chopped

For the Dressing:

- 3 tablespoons olive oil
- 2 tablespoons lime juice
- 1 teaspoon ground cumin
- 1 teaspoon chili powder
- Salt and pepper to taste

Instructions:

In a large bowl, combine the cooked quinoa, black beans, corn, cherry tomatoes, red bell pepper, red onion, and cilantro.

In a small bowl, whisk together the olive oil, lime juice, ground cumin, chili powder, salt, and pepper to create the dressing.

Pour the dressing over the quinoa and black bean mixture. Toss gently to combine, ensuring the salad is well coated with the dressing.

Taste and adjust the seasoning if necessary.

Refrigerate the salad for at least 30 minutes to allow the flavors to meld.

Before serving, give the salad a gentle toss and garnish with additional cilantro if desired.

This Quinoa and Black Bean Salad is not only delicious but also packed with protein and nutrients, making it a perfect option for a light and nutritious meal. Enjoy!

Roasted Vegetable Buddha Bowl

Ingredients:

For the Roasted Vegetables:

- 1 sweet potato, peeled and cubed
- 1 zucchini, sliced
- 1 red bell pepper, sliced
- 1 cup cherry tomatoes, halved
- 1 tablespoon olive oil
- Salt and pepper to taste
- 1 teaspoon smoked paprika
- 1 teaspoon garlic powder
- 1 teaspoon dried thyme

For the Buddha Bowl:

- 1 cup cooked quinoa or rice
- 1 cup mixed greens (spinach, kale, or arugula)
- 1/2 cup hummus
- 1/4 cup feta cheese, crumbled (optional)
- Lemon wedges for serving

Instructions:

Preheat the oven to 400°F (200°C).
In a large bowl, toss the sweet potato, zucchini, red bell pepper, and cherry tomatoes with olive oil, salt, pepper, smoked paprika, garlic powder, and dried thyme until well coated.
Spread the vegetables in a single layer on a baking sheet lined with parchment paper.
Roast in the preheated oven for 25-30 minutes or until the vegetables are tender and slightly caramelized, tossing halfway through.
While the vegetables are roasting, assemble the Buddha Bowl. Divide the cooked quinoa or rice among serving bowls.
Top each bowl with the roasted vegetables, mixed greens, and a dollop of hummus.
Sprinkle with crumbled feta cheese if desired.
Serve the Buddha Bowl with lemon wedges on the side for a burst of freshness.

Enjoy your Roasted Vegetable Buddha Bowl, a nourishing and flavorful dish that brings together a variety of textures and tastes!

Spinach and Feta Stuffed Chicken Breast

Ingredients:

For the Chicken:

- 4 boneless, skinless chicken breasts
- Salt and pepper to taste
- 1 teaspoon garlic powder
- 1 teaspoon paprika
- 1 tablespoon olive oil

For the Spinach and Feta Filling:

- 2 cups fresh spinach, chopped
- 1/2 cup feta cheese, crumbled
- 1/4 cup sun-dried tomatoes, chopped
- 2 cloves garlic, minced
- Salt and pepper to taste

For the Creamy Garlic Sauce:

- 1/2 cup Greek yogurt or sour cream
- 2 tablespoons mayonnaise
- 2 cloves garlic, minced
- 1 tablespoon lemon juice
- Salt and pepper to taste

Instructions:

Preheat the oven to 375°F (190°C).
In a pan, heat olive oil over medium heat. Add chopped spinach and minced garlic. Sauté until the spinach wilts. Remove from heat and let it cool.
In a bowl, mix together the cooked spinach, crumbled feta, chopped sun-dried tomatoes, salt, and pepper. This is your stuffing mixture.
Pat the chicken breasts dry and season both sides with salt, pepper, garlic powder, and paprika.
Cut a pocket into the side of each chicken breast. Be careful not to cut all the way through.

Stuff each chicken breast with the spinach and feta mixture, pressing down gently to close the pocket.

In an oven-safe skillet, heat olive oil over medium-high heat. Sear the stuffed chicken breasts for 2-3 minutes on each side, or until golden brown.

Transfer the skillet to the preheated oven and bake for 20-25 minutes, or until the chicken reaches an internal temperature of 165°F (74°C).

While the chicken is baking, prepare the creamy garlic sauce by mixing together Greek yogurt (or sour cream), mayonnaise, minced garlic, lemon juice, salt, and pepper in a bowl.

Once the chicken is cooked, remove it from the oven and let it rest for a few minutes.

Serve the Spinach and Feta Stuffed Chicken Breast drizzled with creamy garlic sauce.

Enjoy your delicious and flavorful stuffed chicken breast!

Mediterranean Chickpea Salad

Ingredients:

For the Salad:

- 2 cans (15 oz each) chickpeas, drained and rinsed
- 1 cucumber, diced
- 1 cup cherry tomatoes, halved
- 1 red bell pepper, diced
- 1/2 red onion, finely chopped
- 1/2 cup Kalamata olives, sliced
- 1/2 cup crumbled feta cheese
- 1/4 cup fresh parsley, chopped

For the Dressing:

- 1/4 cup extra-virgin olive oil
- 3 tablespoons red wine vinegar
- 1 teaspoon dried oregano
- 1 teaspoon honey (optional)
- Salt and pepper to taste

Instructions:

In a large bowl, combine the chickpeas, cucumber, cherry tomatoes, red bell pepper, red onion, olives, feta cheese, and parsley.
In a small bowl or jar, whisk together the olive oil, red wine vinegar, dried oregano, honey (if using), salt, and pepper to make the dressing.
Pour the dressing over the chickpea mixture and toss gently until everything is well coated.
Taste and adjust the seasoning if needed.
Allow the salad to marinate in the refrigerator for at least 30 minutes to let the flavors meld.
Before serving, give the salad a gentle toss and garnish with extra feta cheese and parsley if desired.
Serve chilled as a refreshing side dish or a light main course.

This Mediterranean Chickpea Salad is not only colorful and vibrant but also packed with Mediterranean flavors. Enjoy!

Sweet Potato and Kale Hash

Ingredients:

- 2 large sweet potatoes, peeled and diced
- 1 bunch of kale, stems removed and leaves chopped
- 1 onion, finely chopped
- 2 cloves garlic, minced
- 2 tablespoons olive oil
- 1 teaspoon smoked paprika
- 1/2 teaspoon ground cumin
- Salt and pepper to taste
- Pinch of red pepper flakes (optional)
- 4 eggs (optional, for serving)

Instructions:

In a large skillet, heat olive oil over medium heat.
Add chopped onions and sauté until they become translucent, about 3-4 minutes.
Add minced garlic and sauté for an additional 1-2 minutes until fragrant.
Add diced sweet potatoes to the skillet. Cook for about 10-15 minutes, stirring occasionally, until sweet potatoes are tender and lightly browned.
Add chopped kale to the skillet and cook until it wilts and becomes tender, about 3-5 minutes.
Season the mixture with smoked paprika, ground cumin, salt, pepper, and red pepper flakes if using. Stir well to combine.
If desired, create small wells in the hash and crack eggs into them. Cover the skillet with a lid and cook until the eggs are cooked to your liking, about 5-7 minutes for a slightly runny yolk.
Alternatively, you can serve the hash as a side dish without eggs.
Taste and adjust the seasoning if needed.
Serve the Sweet Potato and Kale Hash hot, and if you've added eggs, make sure to spoon some of the hash with the eggs onto each plate.

This Sweet Potato and Kale Hash makes for a hearty and nutritious breakfast or brunch option.

Enjoy!

Shrimp and Avocado Lettuce Wraps

Ingredients:

For the Shrimp:

- 1 pound large shrimp, peeled and deveined
- 1 tablespoon olive oil
- 2 cloves garlic, minced
- 1 teaspoon chili powder
- Salt and pepper to taste
- Juice of 1 lime

For the Lettuce Wraps:

- Large lettuce leaves (such as iceberg or butter lettuce)
- 2 avocados, sliced
- 1 cup cherry tomatoes, halved
- 1/4 cup red onion, finely chopped
- Fresh cilantro, chopped, for garnish

For the Sauce:

- 1/4 cup mayonnaise
- 1 tablespoon Sriracha sauce (adjust to taste)
- 1 tablespoon fresh lime juice
- Salt to taste

Instructions:

In a bowl, toss the shrimp with olive oil, minced garlic, chili powder, salt, pepper, and lime juice. Let it marinate for about 15-20 minutes.
Heat a skillet over medium-high heat. Add the marinated shrimp and cook for 2-3 minutes per side or until they are opaque and cooked through.
In a small bowl, mix together the mayonnaise, Sriracha sauce, lime juice, and salt to create the sauce.
Assemble the lettuce wraps: Place a spoonful of shrimp onto each lettuce leaf, top with sliced avocado, cherry tomatoes, and red onion.
Drizzle the sauce over the filling and garnish with chopped cilantro.
Serve immediately and enjoy these Shrimp and Avocado Lettuce Wraps.

These wraps are not only delicious but also a light and refreshing option for a quick meal or appetizer.

Teriyaki Tofu Stir-Fry

Ingredients:

For the Teriyaki Sauce:

- 1/4 cup soy sauce
- 2 tablespoons mirin (Japanese sweet rice wine)
- 1 tablespoon rice vinegar
- 1 tablespoon brown sugar
- 1 teaspoon sesame oil
- 1 teaspoon cornstarch mixed with 1 tablespoon water (optional for thickening)

For the Stir-Fry:

- 14 oz (400g) extra-firm tofu, pressed and cubed
- 2 tablespoons vegetable oil
- 1 bell pepper, thinly sliced
- 1 carrot, julienned
- 1 cup broccoli florets
- 1 cup snap peas, trimmed
- 2 cloves garlic, minced
- 1 tablespoon ginger, grated
- 2 green onions, sliced
- Sesame seeds for garnish
- Cooked rice or noodles for serving

Instructions:

In a small bowl, whisk together the soy sauce, mirin, rice vinegar, brown sugar, sesame oil, and cornstarch-water mixture. Set aside.

Press the tofu to remove excess water. Cut the tofu into cubes.

Heat 1 tablespoon of vegetable oil in a large wok or skillet over medium-high heat. Add the tofu cubes and cook until all sides are golden brown. Remove tofu from the pan and set aside.

In the same pan, add another tablespoon of oil. Add minced garlic and grated ginger. Stir-fry for about 30 seconds until fragrant.

Add sliced bell pepper, julienned carrot, broccoli florets, and snap peas to the pan. Stir-fry for 3-4 minutes until the vegetables are tender-crisp.

Return the cooked tofu to the pan with the vegetables.

Pour the teriyaki sauce over the tofu and vegetables. Toss everything together until well coated and heated through.
Add sliced green onions and stir for an additional 1-2 minutes.
Serve the Teriyaki Tofu Stir-Fry over cooked rice or noodles.
Garnish with sesame seeds and additional green onions if desired.

Enjoy this flavorful and nutritious Teriyaki Tofu Stir-Fry!

Lemon Garlic Roasted Chicken Thighs

Ingredients:

- 4-6 bone-in, skin-on chicken thighs
- Salt and black pepper to taste
- 1 teaspoon paprika
- 4 cloves garlic, minced
- Zest of 1 lemon
- Juice of 1 lemon
- 2 tablespoons olive oil
- 1 teaspoon dried thyme (or 1 tablespoon fresh thyme)
- 1 teaspoon dried rosemary (or 1 tablespoon fresh rosemary)
- Lemon slices for garnish (optional)
- Fresh parsley, chopped, for garnish

Instructions:

Preheat your oven to 425°F (220°C).
Pat the chicken thighs dry with paper towels. Season them generously with salt, black pepper, and paprika.
In a small bowl, mix together minced garlic, lemon zest, lemon juice, olive oil, dried thyme, and dried rosemary.
Place the chicken thighs in a baking dish or on a baking sheet lined with parchment paper.
Brush the chicken thighs with the lemon-garlic mixture, ensuring they are well coated.
If desired, place lemon slices on top of each chicken thigh for extra flavor.
Roast in the preheated oven for 30-35 minutes or until the internal temperature reaches 165°F (74°C) and the skin is golden brown and crispy.
If using fresh herbs, sprinkle them over the chicken during the last 5 minutes of cooking.
Remove the chicken from the oven and let it rest for a few minutes.
Garnish with fresh parsley and serve the Lemon Garlic Roasted Chicken Thighs with your favorite sides.

This recipe results in flavorful and juicy chicken thighs with a delightful combination of lemon and garlic. Enjoy!

Cauliflower Fried Rice

Ingredients:

- 1 medium-sized cauliflower, grated or finely chopped (or use pre-riced cauliflower)
- 2 tablespoons vegetable oil
- 2 cloves garlic, minced
- 1 teaspoon ginger, grated
- 1 cup mixed vegetables (e.g., peas, carrots, corn, and diced bell peppers)
- 2 eggs, beaten
- 3 tablespoons soy sauce (or tamari for a gluten-free option)
- 1 tablespoon sesame oil
- 2 green onions, sliced
- Salt and pepper to taste
- Optional: Cooked and diced protein of your choice (e.g., chicken, shrimp, tofu)

Instructions:

If you haven't already, grate or finely chop the cauliflower into rice-sized pieces. You can also use a food processor for this step.

Heat vegetable oil in a large skillet or wok over medium heat.

Add minced garlic and grated ginger to the pan. Sauté for about 30 seconds until fragrant.

Add the mixed vegetables to the pan and stir-fry for 3-4 minutes until they are slightly tender.

Push the vegetables to one side of the pan and pour the beaten eggs into the empty side. Scramble the eggs until cooked through.

Combine the cooked eggs with the vegetables in the pan.

Add the riced cauliflower to the pan. Stir well to combine with the vegetables and eggs.

Pour soy sauce and sesame oil over the cauliflower mixture. Stir-fry for an additional 3-5 minutes, ensuring everything is well-coated and heated through.

If using a protein source, add the cooked and diced protein to the pan and mix well.

Season with salt and pepper to taste. Adjust the soy sauce and sesame oil if needed.

Stir in sliced green onions and cook for an additional minute.

Serve the Cauliflower Fried Rice hot, garnished with additional green onions if desired.

Enjoy this flavorful and low-carb alternative to traditional fried rice!

Blackened Tilapia Tacos

Ingredients:

For Blackened Tilapia:

- 4 tilapia fillets
- 2 tablespoons olive oil
- 1 tablespoon paprika
- 1 teaspoon onion powder
- 1 teaspoon garlic powder
- 1 teaspoon dried thyme
- 1 teaspoon dried oregano
- 1/2 teaspoon cayenne pepper (adjust to taste)
- 1/2 teaspoon salt
- 1/2 teaspoon black pepper
- 1/2 teaspoon cumin
- Juice of 1 lime

For Tacos:

- 8 small corn or flour tortillas
- Shredded lettuce
- Diced tomatoes
- Sliced red onion
- Sliced avocado
- Fresh cilantro, chopped
- Lime wedges for serving

Optional Sauce:

- 1/2 cup Greek yogurt or sour cream
- 1 tablespoon lime juice
- 1 teaspoon hot sauce (adjust to taste)
- Salt and pepper to taste

Instructions:

Preheat your oven to 375°F (190°C).
In a small bowl, mix together paprika, onion powder, garlic powder, thyme, oregano, cayenne pepper, salt, black pepper, and cumin to create the blackening spice mix.

Brush tilapia fillets with olive oil and rub the blackening spice mix on both sides of each fillet.
Heat a skillet over medium-high heat. Add the tilapia fillets and cook for 2-3 minutes on each side until blackened and cooked through. Squeeze lime juice over the fillets during cooking.
In the oven, warm the tortillas according to package instructions.
Assemble the tacos: Place a blackened tilapia fillet in the center of each tortilla. Top with shredded lettuce, diced tomatoes, sliced red onion, sliced avocado, and chopped cilantro.
If desired, mix together the optional sauce ingredients in a small bowl.
Drizzle the sauce over the tacos or serve it on the side.
Serve the Blackened Tilapia Tacos with lime wedges for squeezing over the top.

Enjoy these flavorful and zesty Blackened Tilapia Tacos!

Caprese Zucchini Noodles

Ingredients:

- 4 medium zucchini, spiralized into noodles
- 1 pint cherry tomatoes, halved
- 1 cup fresh mozzarella balls (bocconcini), halved
- 1/4 cup fresh basil leaves, torn
- 3 tablespoons extra-virgin olive oil
- 2 tablespoons balsamic glaze
- Salt and black pepper to taste
- Optional: Pine nuts for garnish

Instructions:

Spiralize the zucchini into noodles using a spiralizer. If you don't have a spiralizer, you can use a vegetable peeler to create long, thin ribbons.
In a large mixing bowl, combine the zucchini noodles, halved cherry tomatoes, and mozzarella balls.
Drizzle extra-virgin olive oil and balsamic glaze over the zucchini noodles and toss gently to coat.
Season the mixture with salt and black pepper to taste. Toss again to combine.
Add torn fresh basil leaves to the bowl and gently toss one more time.
Optional: Toast pine nuts in a dry skillet over medium heat for a couple of minutes until they become golden brown. Sprinkle them over the zucchini noodles for added crunch.
Serve the Caprese Zucchini Noodles in individual bowls, ensuring each portion has a good mix of zucchini noodles, cherry tomatoes, mozzarella, and basil.
Optionally, drizzle a bit more balsamic glaze on top before serving.

This Caprese Zucchini Noodles dish is a fresh and healthy alternative to traditional pasta, perfect for a light lunch or dinner. Enjoy!

Turkey and Vegetable Skewers

Ingredients:

For the Marinade:

- 1/4 cup olive oil
- 2 tablespoons soy sauce
- 1 tablespoon honey
- 2 cloves garlic, minced
- 1 teaspoon dried oregano
- 1 teaspoon paprika
- Salt and pepper to taste

For the Skewers:

- 1 pound turkey breast or turkey tenderloin, cut into cubes
- 1 red bell pepper, cut into chunks
- 1 yellow bell pepper, cut into chunks
- 1 zucchini, sliced into rounds
- 1 red onion, cut into chunks
- Cherry tomatoes
- Wooden skewers, soaked in water for 30 minutes

Instructions:

In a bowl, whisk together all the marinade ingredients - olive oil, soy sauce, honey, minced garlic, dried oregano, paprika, salt, and pepper.
Cut the turkey into cubes and place them in a resealable plastic bag or shallow dish. Pour half of the marinade over the turkey, making sure it's well coated. Reserve the other half for later.
Marinate the turkey in the refrigerator for at least 30 minutes, or ideally, 2 hours.
Preheat the grill or grill pan over medium-high heat.
Thread the marinated turkey cubes onto the soaked wooden skewers, alternating with the bell peppers, zucchini, red onion, and cherry tomatoes.
Brush the skewers with the reserved marinade.
Grill the skewers for about 10-15 minutes, turning occasionally, until the turkey is cooked through and the vegetables are tender and slightly charred.
Serve the Turkey and Vegetable Skewers hot, garnished with fresh herbs if desired.

These Turkey and Vegetable Skewers make a delicious and healthy meal, perfect for a summer barbecue or a quick weeknight dinner. Enjoy!

Tomato Basil Mozzarella Chicken

Ingredients:

- 4 boneless, skinless chicken breasts
- Salt and black pepper to taste
- 2 tablespoons olive oil
- 4 large tomatoes, sliced
- 1 cup fresh mozzarella cheese, sliced
- 1/2 cup fresh basil leaves
- 2 cloves garlic, minced
- Balsamic glaze for drizzling (optional)

Instructions:

Preheat your oven to 400°F (200°C).
Season the chicken breasts with salt and black pepper.
In a large oven-safe skillet, heat olive oil over medium-high heat.
Sear the chicken breasts for 2-3 minutes on each side, or until golden brown.
Add minced garlic to the skillet and sauté for about 30 seconds until fragrant.
Place tomato slices on top of each chicken breast.
Add fresh mozzarella slices on top of the tomatoes.
Transfer the skillet to the preheated oven and bake for 20-25 minutes, or until the chicken is cooked through and the cheese is melted and bubbly.
Remove the skillet from the oven and top each chicken breast with fresh basil leaves.
If desired, drizzle with balsamic glaze for extra flavor.
Serve the Tomato Basil Mozzarella Chicken hot, directly from the skillet.

Enjoy this delicious and classic combination of flavors!

Greek Yogurt Parfait with Berries

Ingredients:

- 1 cup Greek yogurt (plain or vanilla)
- 1 cup mixed berries (strawberries, blueberries, raspberries)
- 1/4 cup granola
- 1 tablespoon honey or maple syrup (optional)
- Fresh mint leaves for garnish (optional)

Instructions:

In a glass or a bowl, start by layering about 1/4 cup of Greek yogurt at the bottom.
Add a layer of mixed berries on top of the yogurt.
Sprinkle a tablespoon of granola over the berries.
Repeat the layers until the glass or bowl is filled, finishing with a dollop of Greek yogurt on top.
Drizzle honey or maple syrup over the parfait for extra sweetness if desired.
Garnish with fresh mint leaves for a pop of color and added freshness.
Serve the Greek Yogurt Parfait immediately and enjoy!

Feel free to customize this parfait by adding nuts, seeds, or other favorite toppings. It's a nutritious and delightful treat for breakfast, snack, or dessert.

Lentil and Vegetable Soup

Ingredients:

- 1 cup dried green or brown lentils, rinsed and drained
- 1 tablespoon olive oil
- 1 onion, chopped
- 2 carrots, peeled and diced
- 2 celery stalks, diced
- 3 cloves garlic, minced
- 1 teaspoon ground cumin
- 1 teaspoon ground coriander
- 1 teaspoon smoked paprika
- 1 bay leaf
- 1 can (14 oz) diced tomatoes
- 6 cups vegetable or chicken broth
- 2 cups chopped kale or spinach
- Salt and pepper to taste
- Fresh lemon juice (optional, for serving)
- Fresh parsley, chopped, for garnish

Instructions:

In a large pot, heat the olive oil over medium heat. Add the chopped onion, carrots, and celery. Cook for about 5 minutes until the vegetables are softened.
Add minced garlic, ground cumin, ground coriander, smoked paprika, and bay leaf. Stir well and cook for an additional 2 minutes until fragrant.
Add the lentils, diced tomatoes, and broth to the pot. Bring the soup to a boil, then reduce the heat to low and let it simmer for about 25-30 minutes, or until the lentils are tender.
Add chopped kale or spinach to the soup and cook for an additional 5 minutes until the greens are wilted.
Season the soup with salt and pepper to taste. Adjust the seasoning if needed.
Remove the bay leaf before serving.
Optionally, squeeze fresh lemon juice into each bowl just before serving for a burst of freshness.
Garnish with chopped fresh parsley.

Enjoy this wholesome Lentil and Vegetable Soup as a comforting and nutritious meal!

Baked Cod with Herbed Quinoa

Ingredients:

For Baked Cod:

- 4 cod fillets
- 2 tablespoons olive oil
- 1 tablespoon lemon juice
- 2 cloves garlic, minced
- 1 teaspoon dried oregano
- 1 teaspoon dried thyme
- Salt and pepper to taste
- Lemon wedges for serving

For Herbed Quinoa:

- 1 cup quinoa, rinsed
- 2 cups vegetable or chicken broth
- 1 tablespoon olive oil
- 1 teaspoon dried parsley
- 1 teaspoon dried basil
- Salt and pepper to taste

Instructions:

For Baked Cod:

Preheat the oven to 400°F (200°C).
In a small bowl, mix together olive oil, lemon juice, minced garlic, dried oregano, dried thyme, salt, and pepper.
Place the cod fillets in a baking dish. Brush the fillets with the herbed olive oil mixture, coating them evenly.
Bake in the preheated oven for 15-20 minutes, or until the cod is cooked through and flakes easily with a fork.
Optional: Broil the cod for an additional 2-3 minutes to get a golden-brown crust.
Remove from the oven and serve the baked cod with lemon wedges.

For Herbed Quinoa:

In a medium saucepan, combine quinoa and broth. Bring to a boil.

Reduce heat to low, cover, and simmer for 15-20 minutes, or until the quinoa is cooked and the liquid is absorbed.
Fluff the quinoa with a fork and stir in olive oil, dried parsley, dried basil, salt, and pepper.
Serve the herbed quinoa alongside the baked cod.

This Baked Cod with Herbed Quinoa is a balanced and flavorful meal. Enjoy!

Pesto Pasta with Cherry Tomatoes

Ingredients:

- 8 oz (about 225g) pasta (spaghetti, fettuccine, or your choice)
- 1 cup cherry tomatoes, halved
- 1/2 cup grated Parmesan cheese
- 1/3 cup pine nuts, toasted
- 2 cups fresh basil leaves
- 2 cloves garlic
- 1/2 cup extra-virgin olive oil
- Salt and black pepper to taste
- Red pepper flakes (optional, for heat)
- Additional Parmesan for serving

Instructions:

Cook the pasta according to the package instructions until al dente. Reserve about 1/2 cup of pasta cooking water before draining.

While the pasta is cooking, make the pesto. In a food processor, combine fresh basil, garlic, pine nuts, and Parmesan cheese. Pulse until finely chopped.

With the food processor running, slowly pour in the olive oil until the pesto reaches a smooth consistency. Season with salt and pepper to taste. If it's too thick, you can thin it out with a bit of the reserved pasta cooking water.

In a large bowl, toss the cooked pasta with the cherry tomatoes and pesto sauce until everything is well coated.

Season with additional salt, black pepper, and red pepper flakes if desired.

Serve the Pesto Pasta with Cherry Tomatoes topped with additional Parmesan cheese.

This Pesto Pasta is a quick and flavorful dish, perfect for a light and satisfying meal. Enjoy!

Turkey and Quinoa Stuffed Peppers

Ingredients:

- 4 large bell peppers, halved and seeds removed
- 1 cup quinoa, rinsed
- 2 cups low-sodium chicken or vegetable broth
- 1 tablespoon olive oil
- 1 onion, finely chopped
- 2 cloves garlic, minced
- 1 pound ground turkey
- 1 can (14 oz) diced tomatoes, drained
- 1 teaspoon ground cumin
- 1 teaspoon paprika
- 1/2 teaspoon dried oregano
- Salt and pepper to taste
- 1 cup black beans, drained and rinsed
- 1 cup corn kernels (fresh, frozen, or canned)
- 1 cup shredded cheddar or Mexican cheese blend
- Fresh cilantro or parsley for garnish (optional)

Instructions:

Preheat the oven to 375°F (190°C).
In a medium saucepan, bring the quinoa and chicken or vegetable broth to a boil. Reduce heat, cover, and simmer for about 15 minutes, or until the quinoa is cooked and liquid is absorbed.
While the quinoa is cooking, heat olive oil in a large skillet over medium heat. Add chopped onion and sauté until softened, about 3-4 minutes. Add minced garlic and cook for an additional 1 minute.
Add ground turkey to the skillet and cook until browned, breaking it up with a spoon as it cooks.
Stir in diced tomatoes, ground cumin, paprika, dried oregano, salt, and pepper. Cook for another 3-4 minutes.
In a large mixing bowl, combine the cooked quinoa, turkey mixture, black beans, corn, and half of the shredded cheese. Mix well.
Arrange the halved bell peppers in a baking dish. Stuff each pepper half with the turkey and quinoa mixture.
Top each stuffed pepper with the remaining shredded cheese.
Cover the baking dish with aluminum foil and bake in the preheated oven for 25-30 minutes, or until the peppers are tender.
Remove the foil and bake for an additional 5-10 minutes until the cheese is melted and bubbly.

Garnish with fresh cilantro or parsley if desired.

Serve these Turkey and Quinoa Stuffed Peppers with a side of salsa, guacamole, or sour cream for extra flavor. Enjoy!

Asian-inspired Salmon Bowl

Ingredients:

For the Salmon:

- 4 salmon fillets
- 2 tablespoons soy sauce
- 1 tablespoon honey
- 1 tablespoon sesame oil
- 1 tablespoon rice vinegar
- 2 cloves garlic, minced
- 1 teaspoon grated ginger
- 1 tablespoon sesame seeds (optional)
- Sliced green onions for garnish

For the Bowl:

- 2 cups cooked brown rice or quinoa
- 1 cup shredded cabbage
- 1 cucumber, thinly sliced
- 1 carrot, julienned
- 1 avocado, sliced
- 1/4 cup edamame, shelled
- Pickled ginger for garnish
- Soy sauce or teriyaki sauce for drizzling

Instructions:

Preheat the oven to 400°F (200°C).
In a small bowl, whisk together soy sauce, honey, sesame oil, rice vinegar, minced garlic, grated ginger, and sesame seeds.
Place the salmon fillets on a baking sheet lined with parchment paper. Brush the salmon with the prepared marinade.
Bake in the preheated oven for 12-15 minutes or until the salmon is cooked through and flakes easily with a fork.
While the salmon is baking, prepare the bowl ingredients. Divide the cooked brown rice or quinoa among serving bowls.
Arrange shredded cabbage, cucumber slices, julienned carrot, avocado slices, and edamame on top of the rice or quinoa.
Once the salmon is done, place a fillet on each bowl.
Drizzle with additional soy sauce or teriyaki sauce if desired.

Garnish with sliced green onions and pickled ginger.
Serve the Asian-inspired Salmon Bowl immediately and enjoy!

This Salmon Bowl is not only nutritious but also packed with delicious Asian flavors. Feel free to customize the bowl with your favorite vegetables and toppings.

Zucchini Noodles with Pesto and Cherry Tomatoes

Ingredients:

- 4 medium-sized zucchini, spiralized
- 1 cup cherry tomatoes, halved
- 1/2 cup grated Parmesan cheese
- 1/3 cup pine nuts, toasted
- 1 cup fresh basil leaves
- 2 cloves garlic
- 1/2 cup extra-virgin olive oil
- Salt and black pepper to taste
- Red pepper flakes (optional, for heat)
- Additional Parmesan for serving

Instructions:

Make Pesto:
- In a food processor, combine fresh basil, garlic, pine nuts, and Parmesan cheese. Pulse until finely chopped.
- With the food processor running, slowly pour in the olive oil until the pesto reaches a smooth consistency.
- Season with salt and black pepper to taste. If it's too thick, you can thin it out with a bit of water.

Toast Pine Nuts:
- In a dry skillet over medium heat, toast the pine nuts until golden brown and fragrant. Be careful not to burn them. Set aside.

Prepare Zucchini Noodles:
- Spiralize the zucchini into noodles using a spiralizer. If you don't have a spiralizer, you can use a vegetable peeler to create long, thin ribbons.

Assemble the Dish:
- In a large bowl, toss the zucchini noodles with the cherry tomatoes.
- Add the prepared pesto and toss until the noodles are well coated.
- Sprinkle toasted pine nuts over the top.
- Optional: Garnish with red pepper flakes for a bit of heat.

Serve:
- Serve the Zucchini Noodles with Pesto and Cherry Tomatoes in individual bowls.
- Garnish with additional Parmesan cheese if desired.

This dish is a light, fresh, and low-carb alternative to traditional pasta. Enjoy!

Chickpea and Spinach Curry

Ingredients:

- 2 tablespoons vegetable oil
- 1 large onion, finely chopped
- 3 cloves garlic, minced
- 1 tablespoon fresh ginger, grated
- 1 teaspoon ground cumin
- 1 teaspoon ground coriander
- 1 teaspoon turmeric
- 1 teaspoon garam masala
- 1/2 teaspoon chili powder (adjust to taste)
- 1 can (14 oz) chickpeas, drained and rinsed
- 1 can (14 oz) diced tomatoes
- 1 can (14 oz) coconut milk
- 5 cups fresh spinach leaves
- Salt and pepper to taste
- Fresh cilantro, chopped, for garnish
- Cooked rice or naan bread for serving

Instructions:

Heat the vegetable oil in a large skillet or pot over medium heat.
Add chopped onions and sauté until they become translucent, about 5 minutes.
Add minced garlic and grated ginger to the skillet. Sauté for an additional 1-2 minutes until fragrant.
Stir in ground cumin, ground coriander, turmeric, garam masala, and chili powder. Cook the spices for about 1 minute to release their flavors.
Add chickpeas to the skillet and coat them in the spice mixture.
Pour in diced tomatoes with their juices. Stir well and let it simmer for 5-7 minutes.
Add coconut milk to the skillet and let the curry simmer for another 10-15 minutes, allowing the flavors to meld.
Add fresh spinach leaves to the curry and cook until they wilt, about 2-3 minutes.
Season the curry with salt and pepper to taste.
Optional: Garnish the Chickpea and Spinach Curry with chopped fresh cilantro.
Serve the curry over cooked rice or with naan bread.

This Chickpea and Spinach Curry is a delicious and nutritious vegetarian dish. Enjoy!

Roasted Red Pepper and Hummus Wrap

Ingredients:

- 1 large tortilla or wrap
- 1/2 cup hummus (store-bought or homemade)
- 1/2 cup roasted red peppers, sliced
- 1/2 cucumber, thinly sliced
- 1/4 cup feta cheese, crumbled
- Handful of mixed salad greens (e.g., arugula, spinach, or lettuce)
- 1 tablespoon olive oil
- Salt and pepper to taste

Instructions:

Lay the tortilla or wrap on a flat surface.
Spread a generous layer of hummus evenly over the entire surface of the tortilla.
Place the sliced roasted red peppers, cucumber slices, crumbled feta cheese, and mixed salad greens in the center of the tortilla.
Drizzle olive oil over the ingredients and season with salt and pepper to taste.
Fold in the sides of the tortilla and then roll it up tightly from the bottom to create a wrap.
Slice the wrap in half diagonally, if desired.
Serve immediately and enjoy your Roasted Red Pepper and Hummus Wrap!

Feel free to customize the wrap with additional ingredients like olives, cherry tomatoes, or grilled chicken for extra protein. It's a quick and delicious option for a light lunch or dinner.

Honey Mustard Glazed Salmon

Ingredients:

- 4 salmon fillets
- Salt and black pepper to taste
- 2 tablespoons Dijon mustard
- 2 tablespoons honey
- 1 tablespoon whole grain mustard
- 1 tablespoon soy sauce
- 1 tablespoon olive oil
- 2 cloves garlic, minced
- 1 tablespoon fresh lemon juice
- Lemon wedges for serving
- Fresh parsley, chopped, for garnish (optional)

Instructions:

Preheat your oven to 400°F (200°C).

Season the salmon fillets with salt and black pepper.

In a small bowl, whisk together Dijon mustard, honey, whole grain mustard, soy sauce, olive oil, minced garlic, and fresh lemon juice.

Place the salmon fillets on a baking sheet lined with parchment paper or lightly greased.

Brush the honey mustard glaze generously over each salmon fillet.

Bake in the preheated oven for 12-15 minutes, or until the salmon is cooked through and flakes easily with a fork.

Optional: Broil the salmon for an additional 2-3 minutes to get a caramelized crust on top.

Remove from the oven and let it rest for a couple of minutes.

Garnish with chopped fresh parsley if desired and serve the Honey Mustard Glazed Salmon with lemon wedges.

This dish pairs well with steamed vegetables, rice, or a fresh green salad. Enjoy your Honey Mustard Glazed Salmon!

Spaghetti Squash Primavera

Ingredients:

- 1 medium-sized spaghetti squash
- 2 tablespoons olive oil
- 1 small red onion, thinly sliced
- 2 carrots, julienned
- 1 bell pepper (any color), thinly sliced
- 1 zucchini, julienned
- 2 cloves garlic, minced
- 1 cup cherry tomatoes, halved
- 1/2 cup snap peas, trimmed and sliced
- Salt and black pepper to taste
- 1 teaspoon dried oregano
- 1 teaspoon dried basil
- 1/2 cup grated Parmesan cheese
- Fresh basil or parsley for garnish

Instructions:

Preheat your oven to 400°F (200°C).
Cut the spaghetti squash in half lengthwise. Scoop out the seeds and pulp. Place the squash halves, cut side down, on a baking sheet.
Bake the spaghetti squash in the preheated oven for 35-45 minutes, or until the flesh is tender and easily shreds into spaghetti-like strands with a fork.
While the squash is baking, heat olive oil in a large skillet over medium heat.
Add sliced red onion, julienned carrots, and sliced bell pepper to the skillet. Sauté for 3-4 minutes until the vegetables start to soften.
Add julienned zucchini, minced garlic, cherry tomatoes, and sliced snap peas to the skillet. Sauté for an additional 3-4 minutes until the vegetables are tender-crisp.
Season the vegetables with salt, black pepper, dried oregano, and dried basil. Adjust the seasonings to taste.
Once the spaghetti squash is done, use a fork to scrape the flesh into spaghetti-like strands.
Add the spaghetti squash strands to the skillet with the sautéed vegetables. Toss everything together until well combined.
Sprinkle grated Parmesan cheese over the top and continue to toss until the cheese is melted and coats the vegetables.
Garnish with fresh basil or parsley before serving.

Enjoy this Spaghetti Squash Primavera as a light and flavorful alternative to traditional pasta dishes!

Chicken and Broccoli Stir-Fry

Ingredients:

- 1 lb (450g) boneless, skinless chicken breasts, thinly sliced
- 3 cups broccoli florets
- 2 tablespoons soy sauce
- 1 tablespoon oyster sauce
- 1 tablespoon hoisin sauce
- 1 tablespoon cornstarch
- 2 tablespoons water
- 2 tablespoons vegetable oil, divided
- 3 cloves garlic, minced
- 1 tablespoon fresh ginger, grated
- 2 green onions, sliced
- Sesame seeds for garnish (optional)
- Cooked rice for serving

Instructions:

In a bowl, mix together soy sauce, oyster sauce, hoisin sauce, cornstarch, and water to create the stir-fry sauce. Set aside.
Heat 1 tablespoon of vegetable oil in a wok or large skillet over medium-high heat.
Add the sliced chicken to the pan and stir-fry until browned and cooked through. Remove the cooked chicken from the pan and set aside.
In the same pan, add another tablespoon of oil. Stir in minced garlic and grated ginger, sautéing for about 30 seconds until fragrant.
Add broccoli florets to the pan and stir-fry for 3-4 minutes until they are tender-crisp.
Return the cooked chicken to the pan with the broccoli.
Pour the prepared stir-fry sauce over the chicken and broccoli. Toss everything together until well coated and heated through.
Add sliced green onions to the stir-fry and toss for an additional 1-2 minutes.
Optional: Garnish with sesame seeds for extra flavor and texture.
Serve the Chicken and Broccoli Stir-Fry over cooked rice.

This Chicken and Broccoli Stir-Fry is a simple and flavorful dish that can be prepared in no time.

Enjoy!

Avocado and Black Bean Quesadillas

Ingredients:

- 4 large flour tortillas
- 1 can (15 oz) black beans, drained and rinsed
- 2 ripe avocados, sliced
- 1 cup shredded cheddar or Monterey Jack cheese
- 1/2 cup diced tomatoes
- 1/4 cup finely chopped red onion
- 1/4 cup chopped fresh cilantro
- 1 lime, cut into wedges
- Salt and pepper to taste
- Olive oil or cooking spray for grilling

Instructions:

In a bowl, mash the black beans with a fork or potato masher. Season with salt and pepper to taste.
Lay out four tortillas on a flat surface.
Spread an even layer of mashed black beans on two of the tortillas.
Top the black beans with sliced avocado, shredded cheese, diced tomatoes, chopped red onion, and cilantro.
Place the remaining two tortillas on top to form quesadillas.
Heat a large skillet or griddle over medium heat. Lightly brush one side of each quesadilla with olive oil or use cooking spray.
Place the quesadillas, oiled side down, in the skillet or on the griddle.
Cook for 3-4 minutes on each side or until the tortillas are golden brown, and the cheese is melted.
Remove from the skillet and let them rest for a minute before slicing.
Serve the Avocado and Black Bean Quesadillas warm with lime wedges on the side.

These quesadillas are a flavorful and satisfying meal, perfect for a quick lunch or dinner. Enjoy!

Brussels Sprouts and Bacon Hash

Ingredients:

- 4 cups Brussels sprouts, trimmed and halved
- 6 slices bacon, chopped
- 1 onion, finely chopped
- 2 cloves garlic, minced
- 1 teaspoon dried thyme
- Salt and black pepper to taste
- 1 tablespoon olive oil
- 1 tablespoon balsamic vinegar (optional)
- Grated Parmesan cheese for garnish (optional)
- Fried or poached eggs (optional, for serving)

Instructions:

In a large skillet, cook the chopped bacon over medium heat until crispy. Remove bacon from the skillet and set aside.
In the same skillet, add olive oil and chopped onion. Sauté until the onion is softened, about 3-4 minutes.
Add minced garlic to the skillet and cook for an additional 30 seconds until fragrant.
Add halved Brussels sprouts to the skillet, cut side down. Cook for 5-7 minutes, allowing the Brussels sprouts to develop a golden brown crust.
Stir in dried thyme, salt, and black pepper to taste.
Add the cooked bacon back to the skillet and toss everything together.
If using, drizzle balsamic vinegar over the Brussels sprouts and toss to coat.
Cook for an additional 2-3 minutes until the Brussels sprouts are tender but still have a slight crunch.
Optional: Top the Brussels Sprouts and Bacon Hash with grated Parmesan cheese.
Serve the hash on its own or with fried or poached eggs on top.

Enjoy this flavorful Brussels Sprouts and Bacon Hash as a tasty side dish or a hearty breakfast!

Lemon Herb Grilled Shrimp

Ingredients:

- 1 pound large shrimp, peeled and deveined
- 2 tablespoons olive oil
- 3 tablespoons fresh lemon juice
- 2 cloves garlic, minced
- 1 teaspoon dried oregano
- 1 teaspoon dried thyme
- 1 teaspoon paprika
- Salt and black pepper to taste
- Lemon wedges for serving
- Fresh parsley, chopped, for garnish

Instructions:

In a bowl, whisk together olive oil, fresh lemon juice, minced garlic, dried oregano, dried thyme, paprika, salt, and black pepper to create the marinade.
Place the cleaned shrimp in a resealable plastic bag or a shallow dish.
Pour the marinade over the shrimp, making sure they are well coated. Seal the bag or cover the dish and refrigerate for at least 30 minutes, allowing the flavors to meld.
Preheat the grill to medium-high heat.
Thread the marinated shrimp onto skewers.
Grill the shrimp for 2-3 minutes per side, or until they are opaque and cooked through. Be careful not to overcook, as shrimp cook quickly.
Remove the shrimp skewers from the grill.
Serve the Lemon Herb Grilled Shrimp hot, garnished with chopped fresh parsley and lemon wedges on the side.

This Lemon Herb Grilled Shrimp makes a delightful appetizer or main dish. Enjoy!

Ratatouille with Quinoa

Ingredients:

- 1 cup quinoa, rinsed
- 2 cups water or vegetable broth
- 2 tablespoons olive oil
- 1 onion, diced
- 2 cloves garlic, minced
- 1 eggplant, diced
- 1 zucchini, diced
- 1 yellow bell pepper, diced
- 1 red bell pepper, diced
- 2 tomatoes, diced
- 1 can (14 oz) diced tomatoes, undrained
- 1 teaspoon dried thyme
- 1 teaspoon dried rosemary
- Salt and black pepper to taste
- Fresh basil, chopped, for garnish

Instructions:

In a medium saucepan, combine quinoa and water or vegetable broth. Bring to a boil, then reduce heat to low, cover, and simmer for 15-20 minutes, or until the quinoa is cooked and the liquid is absorbed.

While the quinoa is cooking, heat olive oil in a large skillet or pot over medium heat.

Add diced onion and minced garlic. Sauté for about 3-4 minutes until the onions are softened.

Add diced eggplant, zucchini, and bell peppers to the skillet. Cook for another 5-7 minutes until the vegetables start to soften.

Stir in diced fresh tomatoes, canned diced tomatoes (undrained), dried thyme, dried rosemary, salt, and black pepper. Mix well.

Simmer the ratatouille mixture over medium-low heat for 20-25 minutes, stirring occasionally, until the vegetables are tender and the flavors have melded.

Taste and adjust the seasonings if needed.

Serve the ratatouille over cooked quinoa.

Garnish with chopped fresh basil just before serving.

Enjoy this Ratatouille with Quinoa as a nutritious and satisfying meal!

Cilantro Lime Chicken Skewers

Ingredients:

- 1.5 lbs (about 700g) boneless, skinless chicken breasts, cut into cubes
- 1/4 cup fresh cilantro, chopped
- 3 tablespoons olive oil
- Zest of 2 limes
- Juice of 2 limes
- 2 cloves garlic, minced
- 1 teaspoon ground cumin
- 1 teaspoon paprika
- 1 teaspoon chili powder (adjust to taste)
- Salt and black pepper to taste
- Wooden skewers, soaked in water for 30 minutes

Instructions:

In a bowl, whisk together chopped cilantro, olive oil, lime zest, lime juice, minced garlic, ground cumin, paprika, chili powder, salt, and black pepper to create the marinade.

Place the cubed chicken in a resealable plastic bag or a shallow dish.

Pour the marinade over the chicken, ensuring all pieces are well coated. Seal the bag or cover the dish and refrigerate for at least 30 minutes, allowing the flavors to infuse.

Preheat your grill or grill pan over medium-high heat.

Thread the marinated chicken cubes onto the soaked wooden skewers.

Grill the chicken skewers for 6-8 minutes, turning occasionally, or until the chicken is fully cooked and has a nice char on the outside.

Serve the Cilantro Lime Chicken Skewers hot, garnished with additional cilantro and lime wedges on the side.

These Cilantro Lime Chicken Skewers are perfect for a summer barbecue or a quick weeknight dinner. Enjoy!

Sweet Potato and Black Bean Enchiladas

Ingredients:

For the Filling:

- 2 medium-sized sweet potatoes, peeled and diced
- 1 can (15 oz) black beans, drained and rinsed
- 1 cup corn kernels (fresh, frozen, or canned)
- 1 small red onion, finely chopped
- 2 cloves garlic, minced
- 1 teaspoon ground cumin
- 1 teaspoon chili powder
- Salt and black pepper to taste
- 1 tablespoon olive oil

For the Enchilada Sauce:

- 2 cups tomato sauce
- 1 teaspoon ground cumin
- 1 teaspoon chili powder
- 1/2 teaspoon garlic powder
- Salt to taste

For Assembly:

- 8 small flour or corn tortillas
- 1.5 cups shredded cheese (cheddar, Monterey Jack, or a blend)
- Fresh cilantro, chopped, for garnish
- Avocado slices for serving (optional)
- Sour cream or Greek yogurt for serving (optional)

Instructions:

Prepare the Filling:
- Preheat the oven to 375°F (190°C).
- In a large skillet, heat olive oil over medium heat. Add chopped red onion and minced garlic, sautéing until softened.
- Add diced sweet potatoes, black beans, corn, ground cumin, chili powder, salt, and black pepper. Cook until sweet potatoes are tender, about 10-12 minutes.

Prepare the Enchilada Sauce:

- In a saucepan, combine tomato sauce, ground cumin, chili powder, garlic powder, and salt. Simmer for 5-7 minutes, allowing the flavors to meld. Adjust seasoning to taste.

Assemble the Enchiladas:
- Pour a thin layer of enchilada sauce into the bottom of a baking dish.
- Warm the tortillas briefly to make them pliable.
- Spoon the sweet potato and black bean filling into each tortilla, roll them up, and place them seam side down in the baking dish.
- Pour the remaining enchilada sauce over the top and sprinkle with shredded cheese.

Bake:
- Bake in the preheated oven for 20-25 minutes, or until the cheese is melted and bubbly.

Serve:
- Garnish the Sweet Potato and Black Bean Enchiladas with chopped cilantro.
- Serve with avocado slices and a dollop of sour cream or Greek yogurt if desired.

Enjoy these flavorful and satisfying Sweet Potato and Black Bean Enchiladas!

Greek Salad with Grilled Chicken

Ingredients:

For the Grilled Chicken:

- 4 boneless, skinless chicken breasts
- 2 tablespoons olive oil
- 2 teaspoons dried oregano
- 1 teaspoon garlic powder
- Salt and black pepper to taste
- Juice of 1 lemon

For the Greek Salad:

- 1 large cucumber, diced
- 4 medium tomatoes, diced
- 1 red onion, thinly sliced
- 1 cup Kalamata olives, pitted and halved
- 1 cup feta cheese, crumbled
- 1 cup cherry tomatoes, halved
- 1/2 cup fresh parsley, chopped

For the Dressing:

- 1/4 cup extra-virgin olive oil
- 2 tablespoons red wine vinegar
- 1 teaspoon dried oregano
- Salt and black pepper to taste

Instructions:

Grill the Chicken:
- In a bowl, mix olive oil, dried oregano, garlic powder, salt, black pepper, and lemon juice.
- Coat chicken breasts with the marinade and let them marinate for at least 30 minutes.
- Preheat the grill to medium-high heat. Grill the chicken for about 6-8 minutes per side or until cooked through. Let it rest for a few minutes before slicing.

Prepare the Salad:
- In a large bowl, combine diced cucumber, diced tomatoes, thinly sliced red onion, Kalamata olives, crumbled feta cheese, cherry tomatoes, and chopped fresh parsley.

Make the Dressing:
- In a small bowl, whisk together extra-virgin olive oil, red wine vinegar, dried oregano, salt, and black pepper.

Assemble the Salad:
- Drizzle the dressing over the salad and toss gently to combine.

Serve:
- Arrange the sliced grilled chicken on top of the Greek Salad.
- Optionally, garnish with additional feta cheese and fresh parsley.

Enjoy this Greek Salad with Grilled Chicken as a light and satisfying meal!

Teriyaki Vegetable Stir-Fry

Ingredients:

For the Stir-Fry Sauce:

- 1/4 cup soy sauce
- 2 tablespoons teriyaki sauce
- 1 tablespoon honey or maple syrup
- 1 tablespoon rice vinegar
- 1 teaspoon sesame oil
- 1 teaspoon cornstarch

For the Stir-Fry:

- 2 tablespoons vegetable oil
- 1 tablespoon fresh ginger, minced
- 3 cloves garlic, minced
- 1 broccoli crown, cut into florets
- 1 red bell pepper, thinly sliced
- 1 yellow bell pepper, thinly sliced
- 1 carrot, julienned
- 1 zucchini, sliced
- 1 cup snap peas, trimmed
- 1 cup baby corn, halved
- 1 cup mushrooms, sliced
- Sesame seeds for garnish (optional)
- Green onions, chopped, for garnish (optional)
- Cooked rice or noodles for serving

Instructions:

Prepare the Stir-Fry Sauce:
- In a small bowl, whisk together soy sauce, teriyaki sauce, honey or maple syrup, rice vinegar, sesame oil, and cornstarch. Set aside.

Stir-Fry Vegetables:
- Heat vegetable oil in a large wok or skillet over medium-high heat.
- Add minced ginger and garlic, and stir-fry for about 30 seconds until fragrant.

Add Vegetables:
- Add broccoli, red bell pepper, yellow bell pepper, carrot, zucchini, snap peas, baby corn, and mushrooms to the wok. Stir-fry for 5-7 minutes or until the vegetables are tender-crisp.

Sauce and Finish:
- Pour the prepared stir-fry sauce over the vegetables. Toss everything together to coat evenly.
- Cook for an additional 2-3 minutes until the sauce thickens slightly.

Serve:
- Serve the Teriyaki Vegetable Stir-Fry over cooked rice or noodles.
- Garnish with sesame seeds and chopped green onions if desired.

Enjoy this Teriyaki Vegetable Stir-Fry as a delicious and wholesome meal!

Baked Eggplant Parmesan

Ingredients:

- 2 large eggplants, peeled and sliced into 1/2-inch rounds
- 2 cups marinara sauce (store-bought or homemade)
- 2 cups shredded mozzarella cheese
- 1 cup grated Parmesan cheese
- 1 cup breadcrumbs
- 2 teaspoons dried oregano
- 2 teaspoons dried basil
- 1/2 teaspoon garlic powder
- Salt and black pepper to taste
- Fresh basil or parsley, chopped, for garnish

Instructions:

Preheat the Oven:
- Preheat your oven to 400°F (200°C).

Prepare the Eggplant:
- Place the eggplant slices on a paper towel-lined surface. Sprinkle both sides with salt and let them sit for about 15-20 minutes to release excess moisture.
- After 20 minutes, pat the eggplant slices dry with paper towels.

Coat with Breadcrumbs:
- In a shallow dish, mix breadcrumbs with dried oregano, dried basil, garlic powder, salt, and black pepper.
- Dip each eggplant slice into the breadcrumb mixture, ensuring both sides are coated.

Bake the Eggplant:
- Place the breaded eggplant slices on a baking sheet lined with parchment paper.
- Bake in the preheated oven for 15-20 minutes, or until the eggplant is tender and golden brown.

Assemble the Parmesan:
- In a baking dish, spread a thin layer of marinara sauce.
- Arrange a layer of baked eggplant slices on top of the sauce.
- Sprinkle mozzarella and Parmesan cheese over the eggplant.

- Repeat the layers until all the ingredients are used, finishing with a layer of cheese on top.

Bake Until Cheese Melts:
- Bake in the oven for an additional 15-20 minutes, or until the cheese is melted and bubbly.

Garnish and Serve:
- Remove from the oven and let it cool for a few minutes.
- Garnish with chopped fresh basil or parsley before serving.

Serve this Baked Eggplant Parmesan over pasta or with a side of crusty bread for a comforting and satisfying meal!

Turkey and Spinach Meatballs

Ingredients:

- 1 pound ground turkey
- 1 cup fresh spinach, finely chopped
- 1/2 cup breadcrumbs
- 1/4 cup grated Parmesan cheese
- 1/4 cup chopped fresh parsley
- 1 egg
- 2 cloves garlic, minced
- 1 teaspoon dried oregano
- 1/2 teaspoon dried basil
- Salt and black pepper to taste
- Olive oil for greasing

Instructions:

Preheat the Oven:
- Preheat your oven to 375°F (190°C).

Prepare the Meatball Mixture:
- In a large mixing bowl, combine ground turkey, chopped spinach, breadcrumbs, grated Parmesan cheese, chopped parsley, egg, minced garlic, dried oregano, dried basil, salt, and black pepper.
- Mix the ingredients together until well combined.

Shape the Meatballs:
- Take small portions of the mixture and roll them into meatballs, about 1 to 1.5 inches in diameter.

Bake the Meatballs:
- Place the meatballs on a greased or parchment-lined baking sheet.
- Bake in the preheated oven for 20-25 minutes or until the meatballs are cooked through and golden brown.

Serve:
- Remove the meatballs from the oven and let them cool for a few minutes.
- Serve the Turkey and Spinach Meatballs with your favorite sauce, pasta, or as a healthy appetizer.

Feel free to customize this recipe by adding your preferred herbs and spices. These Turkey and Spinach Meatballs are a nutritious option for a satisfying meal!

Quinoa and Kale Stuffed Acorn Squash

Ingredients:

- 2 acorn squash, halved and seeds removed
- 1 cup quinoa, rinsed
- 2 cups vegetable broth or water
- 1 bunch kale, stems removed and leaves chopped
- 1 tablespoon olive oil
- 1 onion, finely chopped
- 2 cloves garlic, minced
- 1 teaspoon dried thyme
- 1/2 teaspoon ground cumin
- Salt and black pepper to taste
- 1/4 cup dried cranberries or raisins
- 1/4 cup chopped pecans or walnuts (optional)
- Fresh parsley, chopped, for garnish

Instructions:

Preheat the Oven:
- Preheat your oven to 400°F (200°C).

Prepare the Acorn Squash:
- Cut the acorn squash in half and remove the seeds.
- Place the squash halves on a baking sheet, cut side up. You may brush the cut sides with a little olive oil and season with salt and pepper if desired.
- Roast in the preheated oven for 30-40 minutes or until the squash is tender when pierced with a fork.

Cook the Quinoa:
- In a saucepan, combine quinoa and vegetable broth or water. Bring to a boil, then reduce heat to low, cover, and simmer for 15-20 minutes, or until the quinoa is cooked and the liquid is absorbed.

Prepare the Filling:
- In a large skillet, heat olive oil over medium heat.
- Add chopped onion and cook until softened, about 3-4 minutes.
- Add minced garlic, chopped kale, dried thyme, ground cumin, salt, and black pepper. Sauté until the kale is wilted.

Combine and Stuff:
- In a large mixing bowl, combine the cooked quinoa, sautéed kale mixture, dried cranberries or raisins, and chopped nuts if using. Mix well.

Stuff the Squash:
- Spoon the quinoa and kale mixture into the roasted acorn squash halves.

Final Bake:

- Return the stuffed squash to the oven and bake for an additional 10-15 minutes, or until the filling is heated through.

Garnish and Serve:
- Remove from the oven and garnish with fresh chopped parsley.
- Serve the Quinoa and Kale Stuffed Acorn Squash halves warm.

This dish makes for a hearty and flavorful vegetarian meal. Enjoy!

Tuna Salad Lettuce Wraps

Ingredients:

- 2 cans (5 oz each) tuna, drained
- 1/4 cup mayonnaise
- 2 tablespoons Greek yogurt or sour cream
- 1 celery stalk, finely diced
- 1/4 red onion, finely diced
- 1 tablespoon Dijon mustard
- 1 tablespoon fresh lemon juice
- Salt and black pepper to taste
- Lettuce leaves for wrapping (butter lettuce or Romaine work well)
- Avocado slices for garnish (optional)
- Cherry tomatoes for garnish (optional)
- Fresh parsley or cilantro, chopped, for garnish (optional)

Instructions:

Prepare the Tuna Salad:
- In a bowl, combine drained tuna, mayonnaise, Greek yogurt or sour cream, diced celery, diced red onion, Dijon mustard, fresh lemon juice, salt, and black pepper.
- Mix well until all ingredients are evenly combined.

Assemble the Lettuce Wraps:
- Spoon a portion of the tuna salad onto each lettuce leaf.

Garnish:
- Garnish the tuna salad with avocado slices, cherry tomatoes, and chopped fresh herbs if desired.

Serve:
- Serve the Tuna Salad Lettuce Wraps immediately.

These lettuce wraps are a light and refreshing option for a quick lunch or a healthy snack. Customize the recipe to your liking by adding ingredients such as diced pickles, shredded carrots, or chopped nuts. Enjoy!

Lemon Rosemary Grilled Swordfish

Ingredients:

- 4 swordfish steaks (about 6 oz each)
- 1/4 cup olive oil
- 2 tablespoons fresh lemon juice
- 2 cloves garlic, minced
- 1 tablespoon fresh rosemary, chopped
- 1 teaspoon lemon zest
- Salt and black pepper to taste
- Lemon wedges for serving
- Fresh parsley, chopped, for garnish (optional)

Instructions:

Prepare the Marinade:
- In a bowl, whisk together olive oil, fresh lemon juice, minced garlic, chopped fresh rosemary, lemon zest, salt, and black pepper.

Marinate the Swordfish:
- Place the swordfish steaks in a shallow dish or a resealable plastic bag.
- Pour the marinade over the swordfish, making sure each steak is well-coated.
- Marinate in the refrigerator for at least 30 minutes, allowing the flavors to infuse.

Preheat the Grill:
- Preheat your grill to medium-high heat.

Grill the Swordfish:
- Remove the swordfish from the marinade and let any excess drip off.
- Grill the swordfish steaks for about 4-5 minutes per side, or until the fish is cooked through and has grill marks. The internal temperature should reach 145°F (63°C).

Serve:
- Transfer the grilled swordfish steaks to a serving platter.
- Garnish with chopped fresh parsley if desired.
- Serve with lemon wedges on the side.

This Lemon Rosemary Grilled Swordfish is a delightful dish that pairs well with a side of grilled vegetables, a salad, or your favorite grain. Enjoy!

Cauliflower and Chickpea Curry

Ingredients:

- 1 cauliflower, cut into florets
- 1 can (15 oz) chickpeas, drained and rinsed
- 1 large onion, finely chopped
- 3 cloves garlic, minced
- 1-inch piece of ginger, grated
- 1 can (14 oz) diced tomatoes
- 1 can (14 oz) coconut milk
- 2 tablespoons curry powder
- 1 teaspoon ground cumin
- 1 teaspoon ground coriander
- 1/2 teaspoon turmeric
- 1/2 teaspoon red chili flakes (adjust to taste)
- Salt and black pepper to taste
- 2 tablespoons vegetable oil
- Fresh cilantro, chopped, for garnish
- Cooked rice or naan bread for serving

Instructions:

Sauté Aromatics:
- In a large pot or deep skillet, heat vegetable oil over medium heat. Add chopped onion and sauté until softened.

Add Garlic and Ginger:
- Add minced garlic and grated ginger to the pot. Sauté for an additional 1-2 minutes until fragrant.

Spices and Tomatoes:
- Stir in curry powder, ground cumin, ground coriander, turmeric, and red chili flakes. Cook for a minute to toast the spices.
- Add diced tomatoes (with their juices) to the pot. Stir well to combine.

Simmer:
- Pour in the coconut milk and bring the mixture to a simmer. Let it cook for about 5-7 minutes, allowing the flavors to meld.

Add Cauliflower and Chickpeas:
- Add cauliflower florets and drained chickpeas to the pot. Stir to coat them with the curry sauce.

Simmer Until Tender:
- Cover the pot and simmer for 15-20 minutes or until the cauliflower is tender.

Adjust Seasoning:
- Season the curry with salt and black pepper to taste. Adjust the spice level if needed.

Serve:
- Serve the Cauliflower and Chickpea Curry over cooked rice or with naan bread.
- Garnish with chopped fresh cilantro.

Enjoy this hearty and flavorful Cauliflower and Chickpea Curry as a delicious vegetarian meal!

Pesto Zoodles with Cherry Tomatoes

Ingredients:

- 4 medium-sized zucchinis, spiralized into zoodles
- 1 cup cherry tomatoes, halved
- 1/2 cup basil pesto (store-bought or homemade)
- 1/4 cup grated Parmesan cheese
- 2 tablespoons pine nuts, toasted
- Salt and black pepper to taste
- Fresh basil, chopped, for garnish (optional)

Instructions:

Prepare Zoodles:
- Spiralize the zucchinis into zoodles using a spiralizer. If you don't have a spiralizer, you can use a vegetable peeler to make ribbon-like zoodles.

Cook Zoodles:
- In a large pan over medium heat, add the zoodles and cook for 2-3 minutes, just until they are heated through but still have a slight crunch. Be careful not to overcook, as zoodles release water when cooked.

Combine with Pesto:
- Add the cherry tomato halves to the pan with the zoodles.
- Stir in the basil pesto, ensuring the zoodles and tomatoes are evenly coated.

Toast Pine Nuts:
- In a separate small pan, toast the pine nuts over medium heat for 2-3 minutes or until they are golden brown. Keep an eye on them, as they can burn quickly.

Assemble:
- Season the Pesto Zoodles with salt and black pepper to taste.
- Plate the zoodles and tomatoes, then sprinkle with grated Parmesan cheese and toasted pine nuts.

Garnish and Serve:
- Optional: Garnish with chopped fresh basil for added flavor and freshness.

Enjoy these Pesto Zoodles with Cherry Tomatoes as a light and satisfying dish. They are a healthy alternative to traditional pasta and can be ready in no time!

Greek Quinoa Salad

Ingredients:

For the Salad:

- 1 cup quinoa, rinsed
- 2 cups water or vegetable broth
- 1 cucumber, diced
- 1 cup cherry tomatoes, halved
- 1/2 cup Kalamata olives, pitted and halved
- 1/2 cup red onion, finely chopped
- 1/2 cup crumbled feta cheese
- 1/4 cup fresh parsley, chopped
- 1/4 cup fresh mint, chopped (optional)

For the Dressing:

- 1/4 cup extra-virgin olive oil
- 2 tablespoons red wine vinegar
- 1 teaspoon dried oregano
- Salt and black pepper to taste
- Juice of 1 lemon

Instructions:

Cook the Quinoa:
- In a medium saucepan, combine quinoa and water or vegetable broth. Bring to a boil, then reduce heat to low, cover, and simmer for 15-20 minutes or until the quinoa is cooked and the liquid is absorbed. Fluff with a fork and let it cool.

Prepare the Vegetables:
- In a large salad bowl, combine the cooked quinoa, diced cucumber, halved cherry tomatoes, Kalamata olives, chopped red onion, crumbled feta cheese, fresh parsley, and optional fresh mint.

Make the Dressing:
- In a small bowl, whisk together extra-virgin olive oil, red wine vinegar, dried oregano, salt, black pepper, and lemon juice.

Combine and Toss:
- Pour the dressing over the salad ingredients in the bowl.

- Toss everything together until well combined.

Chill and Serve:
- Refrigerate the Greek Quinoa Salad for at least 30 minutes before serving to allow the flavors to meld.

Serve:
- Serve the chilled salad on its own or as a side dish.

Enjoy this Greek Quinoa Salad as a refreshing and nutritious meal!

Lemon Garlic Shrimp and Asparagus

Ingredients:

- 1 pound large shrimp, peeled and deveined
- 1 bunch asparagus, tough ends trimmed
- 3 tablespoons olive oil
- 4 cloves garlic, minced
- Zest of 1 lemon
- Juice of 1 lemon
- 1 teaspoon dried oregano
- Salt and black pepper to taste
- Crushed red pepper flakes (optional)
- Fresh parsley, chopped, for garnish

Instructions:

Preheat Oven:
- Preheat your oven to 400°F (200°C).

Prepare Asparagus:
- Place trimmed asparagus on a baking sheet. Drizzle with 1 tablespoon of olive oil and season with salt and pepper. Toss to coat.

Roast Asparagus:
- Roast the asparagus in the preheated oven for 10-12 minutes or until they are tender yet still crisp.

Prepare Shrimp:
- While the asparagus is roasting, in a bowl, mix the shrimp with minced garlic, lemon zest, lemon juice, dried oregano, salt, black pepper, and optional red pepper flakes.

Sauté Shrimp:
- Heat 2 tablespoons of olive oil in a large skillet over medium-high heat. Add the marinated shrimp and cook for 2-3 minutes per side or until they turn pink and opaque.

Combine Shrimp and Asparagus:
- Once the asparagus is done roasting, combine it with the sautéed shrimp in the skillet. Toss everything together to coat in the flavors.

Garnish and Serve:
- Garnish with fresh chopped parsley.
- Serve the Lemon Garlic Shrimp and Asparagus over rice, quinoa, or with a side of crusty bread.

This dish is quick, easy, and bursting with fresh flavors. Enjoy your Lemon Garlic Shrimp and Asparagus!

Mexican Cauliflower Rice Bowl

Ingredients:

For the Cauliflower Rice:

- 1 large head cauliflower, grated or processed into rice-like texture
- 1 tablespoon olive oil
- 1 teaspoon ground cumin
- 1 teaspoon chili powder
- Salt and black pepper to taste

For the Black Bean Salsa:

- 1 can (15 oz) black beans, drained and rinsed
- 1 cup corn kernels (fresh, frozen, or canned)
- 1 cup cherry tomatoes, halved
- 1/4 cup red onion, finely chopped
- 1/4 cup fresh cilantro, chopped
- Juice of 1 lime
- Salt and black pepper to taste

For the Avocado Crema:

- 2 ripe avocados
- 1/4 cup Greek yogurt or sour cream
- Juice of 1 lime
- Salt and black pepper to taste

Additional Toppings:

- Shredded cheese
- Sliced jalapeños
- Sliced radishes
- Lime wedges
- Fresh cilantro, chopped

Instructions:

    Prepare Cauliflower Rice:

- In a large skillet, heat olive oil over medium heat. Add cauliflower rice and sauté for 5-7 minutes until it begins to soften.
- Season with ground cumin, chili powder, salt, and black pepper. Cook for an additional 2-3 minutes. Set aside.

Make Black Bean Salsa:
- In a bowl, combine black beans, corn, cherry tomatoes, red onion, cilantro, lime juice, salt, and black pepper. Toss to combine.

Prepare Avocado Crema:
- In a blender or food processor, combine ripe avocados, Greek yogurt or sour cream, lime juice, salt, and black pepper. Blend until smooth and creamy.

Assemble the Bowl:
- Divide the cauliflower rice among serving bowls.
- Top with black bean salsa, avocado crema, and your choice of additional toppings like shredded cheese, sliced jalapeños, radishes, lime wedges, and chopped cilantro.

Serve:
- Serve the Mexican Cauliflower Rice Bowl immediately, allowing everyone to customize their toppings.

Enjoy this flavorful and healthy Mexican-inspired cauliflower rice bowl!

Roasted Chicken with Brussels Sprouts and Potatoes

Ingredients:

- 4 bone-in, skin-on chicken thighs
- 1 pound Brussels sprouts, trimmed and halved
- 1 pound baby potatoes, halved
- 4 cloves garlic, minced
- 2 tablespoons olive oil
- 1 teaspoon dried thyme
- 1 teaspoon dried rosemary
- 1 teaspoon paprika
- Salt and black pepper to taste
- Lemon wedges for serving
- Fresh parsley, chopped, for garnish

Instructions:

Preheat the Oven:
- Preheat your oven to 425°F (220°C).

Prepare the Chicken:
- Pat the chicken thighs dry with paper towels.
- In a small bowl, mix together minced garlic, olive oil, dried thyme, dried rosemary, paprika, salt, and black pepper.

Coat Chicken:
- Rub the chicken thighs with the garlic and herb mixture, ensuring they are well coated.

Prepare Vegetables:
- In a large bowl, toss halved Brussels sprouts and baby potatoes with a bit of olive oil, salt, and pepper.

Arrange in Baking Dish:
- Arrange the marinated chicken thighs, Brussels sprouts, and potatoes in a baking dish or on a baking sheet, making sure everything is in a single layer.

Roast in the Oven:
- Roast in the preheated oven for 30-40 minutes or until the chicken is cooked through and the vegetables are golden brown and tender. Ensure the chicken reaches an internal temperature of 165°F (74°C).

Garnish and Serve:
- Garnish with chopped fresh parsley and serve the Roasted Chicken with Brussels Sprouts and Potatoes hot.
- Serve with lemon wedges on the side for an extra burst of flavor.

This one-pan meal is perfect for a hassle-free dinner with minimal cleanup. Enjoy!

Veggie and Hummus Wrap

Ingredients:

- Whole-grain or spinach tortillas
- 1 cup hummus (store-bought or homemade)
- 1 cup mixed veggies, thinly sliced or julienned (e.g., bell peppers, cucumbers, carrots, cherry tomatoes, spinach)
- 1/2 cup feta cheese, crumbled (optional)
- 1/4 cup red onion, thinly sliced (optional)
- Fresh herbs, such as parsley or cilantro, chopped
- Salt and black pepper to taste

Instructions:

Prepare the Veggies:
- Slice or julienne your chosen vegetables into thin strips.

Warm the Tortillas (Optional):
- If you prefer warm wraps, you can quickly heat the tortillas in a dry skillet for about 10-15 seconds on each side.

Assemble the Wrap:
- Spread a generous layer of hummus onto the center of each tortilla.

Add Veggies and Cheese:
- Place a handful of mixed veggies on top of the hummus. Add crumbled feta cheese and sliced red onions if using.

Season and Garnish:
- Sprinkle with salt and black pepper to taste.
- Garnish with chopped fresh herbs for added flavor.

Fold and Roll:
- Fold the sides of the tortilla inwards, and then roll it up tightly from the bottom to create a wrap.

Serve:
- Slice the Veggie and Hummus Wrap in half diagonally for easier handling.
- Serve immediately and enjoy!

Feel free to customize your wrap with your favorite veggies, herbs, or additional toppings like avocado slices or a drizzle of balsamic glaze. It's a versatile and nutritious meal that's perfect for a quick lunch or a light dinner.

Shrimp and Vegetable Skewers

Ingredients:

- 1 pound large shrimp, peeled and deveined
- 1 zucchini, sliced into rounds
- 1 bell pepper (any color), cut into chunks
- 1 red onion, cut into chunks
- Cherry tomatoes
- 1/4 cup olive oil
- 2 tablespoons lemon juice
- 2 cloves garlic, minced
- 1 teaspoon dried oregano
- 1 teaspoon paprika
- Salt and black pepper to taste
- Wooden skewers, soaked in water for 30 minutes

Instructions:

Prepare Marinade:
- In a bowl, whisk together olive oil, lemon juice, minced garlic, dried oregano, paprika, salt, and black pepper.

Marinate Shrimp:
- Place the peeled and deveined shrimp in a zip-top bag or shallow dish. Pour half of the marinade over the shrimp and toss to coat. Reserve the remaining marinade for the vegetables.

Prepare Vegetables:
- In another bowl, toss the zucchini rounds, bell pepper chunks, red onion chunks, and cherry tomatoes with the reserved marinade.

Assemble Skewers:
- Thread the marinated shrimp, zucchini, bell pepper, red onion, and cherry tomatoes onto the soaked wooden skewers, alternating between shrimp and vegetables.

Grill or Broil:
- Grill the skewers over medium-high heat for 2-3 minutes per side or until the shrimp is opaque and the vegetables are tender. Alternatively, you can broil them in the oven.

Serve:
- Serve the Shrimp and Vegetable Skewers hot.

- Optionally, garnish with chopped fresh parsley and lemon wedges.

These skewers are not only visually appealing but also packed with flavor. They can be served over rice, quinoa, or a bed of greens for a complete and satisfying meal. Enjoy!

Spinach and Artichoke Stuffed Portobello Mushrooms

Ingredients:

- 4 large portobello mushrooms, stems removed
- 1 tablespoon olive oil
- 2 cups fresh spinach, chopped
- 1 can (14 oz) artichoke hearts, drained and chopped
- 2 cloves garlic, minced
- 1/2 cup cream cheese
- 1/2 cup shredded mozzarella cheese
- 1/4 cup grated Parmesan cheese
- Salt and black pepper to taste
- Fresh parsley, chopped, for garnish

Instructions:

Preheat the Oven:
- Preheat your oven to 375°F (190°C).

Prepare the Portobello Mushrooms:
- Clean the portobello mushrooms with a damp cloth. Remove the stems and gently scrape out the gills with a spoon.

Sauté Spinach and Artichoke:
- In a pan, heat olive oil over medium heat. Add chopped spinach and minced garlic. Cook until the spinach wilts.
- Add chopped artichoke hearts and cook for an additional 2-3 minutes.

Prepare the Filling:
- In a bowl, combine the sautéed spinach and artichoke mixture with cream cheese, mozzarella, Parmesan, salt, and black pepper. Mix well until everything is combined.

Stuff the Portobello Mushrooms:
- Place the cleaned portobello mushrooms on a baking sheet.
- Divide the filling evenly among the mushrooms, pressing it down gently.

Bake in the Oven:
- Bake in the preheated oven for 20-25 minutes, or until the mushrooms are tender and the filling is golden and bubbly.

Garnish and Serve:
- Garnish the stuffed portobello mushrooms with chopped fresh parsley.
- Serve hot as an appetizer or a light meal.

These Spinach and Artichoke Stuffed Portobello Mushrooms are a savory and satisfying dish. Enjoy them on their own or as a side dish to complement your favorite main course!

Coconut Curry Chicken

Ingredients:

- 1.5 pounds boneless, skinless chicken thighs, cut into bite-sized pieces
- 1 can (14 oz) coconut milk
- 1 onion, finely chopped
- 3 cloves garlic, minced
- 1 tablespoon ginger, grated
- 2 tablespoons red curry paste
- 1 tablespoon curry powder
- 1 teaspoon turmeric powder
- 1 bell pepper, sliced
- 1 zucchini, sliced
- 1 carrot, julienned
- 1 cup broccoli florets
- 1 tablespoon vegetable oil
- Salt and pepper to taste
- Fresh cilantro, chopped, for garnish
- Cooked rice for serving

Instructions:

Prepare the Chicken:
- In a large pan or wok, heat vegetable oil over medium heat. Add chopped chicken and cook until browned on all sides. Remove the chicken from the pan and set aside.

Sauté Aromatics:
- In the same pan, add chopped onion, minced garlic, and grated ginger. Sauté until the onion becomes translucent.

Add Curry Paste and Spices:
- Stir in red curry paste, curry powder, and turmeric powder. Cook for 1-2 minutes to release the flavors.

Simmer with Coconut Milk:
- Pour in the coconut milk and bring the mixture to a simmer.

Cook Chicken:
- Add the browned chicken back to the pan. Simmer for 10-15 minutes or until the chicken is cooked through and the sauce has thickened.

Add Vegetables:
- Add sliced bell pepper, zucchini, julienned carrot, and broccoli florets. Cook until the vegetables are tender-crisp.

Season and Garnish:
- Season with salt and pepper to taste. Garnish with chopped fresh cilantro.

Serve:

- Serve the Coconut Curry Chicken over cooked rice.

Enjoy this flavorful and aromatic Coconut Curry Chicken as a comforting and satisfying meal!

Quinoa and Blackberry Salad

Ingredients:

- 1 cup quinoa, rinsed
- 2 cups water or vegetable broth
- 1 cup fresh blackberries
- 1 cup cucumber, diced
- 1/2 cup red onion, finely chopped
- 1/4 cup fresh mint leaves, chopped
- 1/4 cup feta cheese, crumbled (optional)
- 2 tablespoons extra-virgin olive oil
- 1 tablespoon balsamic vinegar
- Salt and black pepper to taste

Instructions:

Cook Quinoa:
- In a medium saucepan, combine quinoa and water or vegetable broth. Bring to a boil, then reduce heat, cover, and simmer for 15-20 minutes or until quinoa is cooked and water is absorbed. Fluff with a fork and let it cool.

Prepare Blackberry Salad:
- In a large bowl, combine cooked quinoa, fresh blackberries, diced cucumber, chopped red onion, and chopped mint.

Add Feta Cheese (Optional):
- If using feta cheese, gently fold it into the salad.

Prepare Dressing:
- In a small bowl, whisk together extra-virgin olive oil and balsamic vinegar. Season with salt and black pepper to taste.

Combine and Toss:
- Drizzle the dressing over the quinoa and blackberry mixture. Gently toss until everything is well coated.

Chill (Optional):
- Allow the salad to chill in the refrigerator for about 30 minutes before serving to let the flavors meld.

Serve:
- Serve the Quinoa and Blackberry Salad as a refreshing side dish or a light meal.

This salad is not only colorful and vibrant but also packed with wholesome ingredients. It's a perfect option for a summer meal or a picnic. Enjoy!

www.ingramcontent.com/pod-product-compliance
Lightning Source LLC
LaVergne TN
LVHW081617060526
838201LV00054B/2281